SPORTS HEROES AND LEGENDS

Alex Rodriguez

D0172259

Read all of the books in this exciting,
action-packed biography series!

Hank Aaron

Muhammad Ali

Lance Armstrong

Barry Bonds

Roberto Clemente

Joe DiMaggio

Tim Duncan

Dale Earnhardt Jr.

Lou Gehrig

Mia Hamm

Tony Hawk

Derek Jeter

Michael Jordan

Sandy Koufax

Michelle Kwan

Mickey Mantle

Shaquille O'Neal

Jesse Owens

Jackie Robinson

Alex Rodriguez

Wilma Rudolph

Babe Ruth

Ichiro Suzuki

Tiger Woods

SPORTS HEROES AND LEGENDS

Alex Rodriguez

by Serena Kappes

BARNES & NOBLE

NEW YORK

*To David—living life with you
is like hitting a home run every day*

Contents

Grand Slam

On June 8, 2005, Alex Rodriguez—nicknamed A-Rod—and the New York Yankees faced the Milwaukee Brewers. The Yankees had lost nine of their last ten games, but A-Rod had a plan to break his team's losing streak and lift their spirits. The third baseman, who was in his second season with the New York Yankees, was two home runs away from making history.

A-Rod had become known as a home-run hitter. Back in 1996, his first full season in the major leagues, he hit thirty-six homers for the Seattle Mariners. In 2002 he slammed an amazing fifty-seven home runs with the Texas Rangers. His home run production went back down to thirty-six in 2004, but by 2005 he was on track to hit his 400th career home run. The fans at Milwaukee's Miller Stadium may not have been cheering for the Yankees, but they were excited to see Alex reach that important milestone.

A-Rod started off strong, turning a pitch from left-hander Chris Capuano into his 399th career home run in the first inning. The round-tripper gave the Yanks two runs and an early lead. During his eighth-inning at bat, A-Rod could practically taste victory. The Yankees had a 10–3 lead, but he was aiming for another run.

Alex steadied himself at the plate as he faced relief pitcher Jorge de la Rosa. The slugger got into his batting stance and waited for the pitch. The ball streaked toward him. Swing . . . connect . . . the ball was out of there! A-Rod had just slugged his 400th homer! As he rounded the bases, he knew he'd made history. At twenty-nine years old, he was the youngest major leaguer to reach the 400 home run mark. Ken Griffey Jr., the next youngest, had scored 400 career homers at age thirty back in 2000.

To top off A-Rod's big day, the Yankees beat the Brewers with a final score of 12–3. Their losing streak had come to a dramatic end. After the game, Alex had time to think about his accomplishment. He was only the thirty-ninth member of the 400 home run club. "It's a special number," A-Rod told reporters. "It was a very special day for me, especially if you do it in a win that we needed most desperately."

No one was prouder than Yankees manager Joe Torre. He had shaken up his players by cancelling their regular batting practice earlier that day. Some reporters joked that the tactic had worked so well, he should cancel batting practice more often. Torre was grateful for A-Rod's role in the team's victory, and he was confident that A-Rod would continue to achieve great things in the future. "The shape he's in, the way he works—who knows where he's going?" Torre said. That's a question many ask about one of baseball's brightest stars.

Chapter One

Born for Baseball

Alexander Emmanuel Rodriguez was born on July 27, 1975. He lived with his family in the Washington Heights section of Manhattan, part of New York City. His parents, Lourdes Navarro Rodriguez and Victor Rodriguez, were immigrants from the Dominican Republic, a Spanish-speaking island nation between Cuba and Puerto Rico. They had come to the United States to find good jobs. Victor opened a shoe store, and Lourdes took a job on an assembly line at General Motors. At home Lourdes and Victor spoke both English and Spanish.

When baby Alex was born, he already had an older sister, Susy, and an older brother, Joe. Even though they didn't have a lot of space, the Rodriguez family's small apartment was filled with love. Alex was extremely close to his father, who babysat him during the day at his shoe store while Lourdes went to work on the assembly line.

Even as a two-year-old, Alex showed an interest in baseball. He carried around a red plastic bat and swung at everything he could, sometimes even breaking household items. To practice his throwing, he would bounce a small rubber ball against a wall for hours on end. That was just fine with Alex's dad, who once had been a catcher with a Dominican baseball league. Victor loved that his youngest child had such an interest in the sport.

Pinball Wizard

As a child, Alex loved to play pinball, which he called "dollar pizza" because it cost one dollar and the local pizza place had a pinball machine. From the time he started walking, he would beg a family member to take him there, with four quarters in hand, so he could play his favorite game.

Victor dreamed of returning to the Dominican Republic one day, and he finally got his chance. By the time Alex was four, Victor had been able to save enough money from his shoe store to move his family back to the island. The Rodriguezes bought a beautiful four-bedroom home one block from the beach in Santo Domingo, the Dominican Republic's capital.

Victor still owned his thriving shoe store. His New York relatives worked there and sent some of the profits to the Rodriguezes.

Four-year-old Alex—who spoke both English and Spanish at home—quickly adjusted to life in Santo Domingo. Plenty of relatives—aunts, uncles, and grandparents—were around, and there was always something to celebrate.

Best of all, the year-round warm weather was perfect for practicing baseball, the island's most popular sport. The Dominican Republic already had contributed a number of major league baseball stars. Juan Marichal, a Hall of Fame pitcher who played in the 1950s and 1960s; home-run star Sammy Sosa; Boston Red Sox left fielder Manny Ramirez; and New York Mets pitcher Pedro Martinez all had come from the Dominican Republic.

Alex learned the ins and outs of the game from his father, who would head out to the backyard with his son every night after dinner and pitch to him. No matter how tired Alex was, he'd swing with all his might. All he wanted to do was play baseball.

By the time he was six, Alex had improved so much that he was playing with boys three and four years older than he was. One day Alex went to the local park to join some friends for a game. As his parents watched, Alex walked with a yellow bat over to a makeshift home plate. As the ball approached, he put all his power into his swing. The ball soared into the air, past the third baseman, and landed in a faraway corner of the field. As

Alex began rounding the bases, an outfielder scooped up the ball and threw it to the shortstop, who rocketed it to home plate. But he was too late—Alex had gotten there before the ball arrived. He had scored his first-ever home run!

Everyone cheered, especially his parents and his team-mates. But no one was more thrilled than Alex. "I was almost crying, I was so happy," he later recalled.

❝When Alex was little, all he wanted me to do was throw him Wiffle balls that he'd hit with a plastic bat. He had that drive from the beginning.❞

—JOE RODRIGUEZ, ALEX'S BROTHER

It was no surprise to his mother that Alex had developed such skill. "He was just very focused from the time he was a child and just wasn't interested in anything else," she recalled. "He didn't care about the sun or the rain. He just had to play ball and would cry if I didn't take him to the park every day."

Usually the youngest kid on the team, Alex started out playing second base. He hated to lose. "If I lost, I would go home crying angry tears," he later wrote. "The whole night I would think of ways we could win the next day."

When Alex was eight, life changed drastically. His family's shoe store in New York wasn't doing well financially. The

Rodriguezes were forced to sell their dream home and leave island living behind. They returned to the United States, where they hoped they could find more financial opportunities than they had in the Dominican Republic.

This time they chose Kendall, Florida, a suburb of Miami. There Victor opened a new shoe store, and Alex tried to adjust to his new life. In the Dominican Republic, he had gotten used to speaking only Spanish in school and with friends and relatives. But at his new school in Florida, everyone spoke English. "My transition from speaking all Spanish in the Dominican Republic to English-based fourth grade proved rocky," Alex later wrote. The adjustment was difficult for Alex, and he had a tough time in school.

Luckily Alex had a much easier time on the sports field. Soon after moving to Kendall, he went to a nearby park to check out practice of a local youth league baseball team. Every day for a month, he sat and watched. Then one day, the team's catcher didn't show up. So the coach, Juan Diego Arteaga, called over to Alex and asked him if he wanted to join in.

That was the start of his baseball career in Kendall. Coach Arteaga became like a second father to Alex. The coach's son, J.D., became Alex's best friend.

Alex would soon need their emotional support. His father was again struggling financially. The Miami shoe store was failing. One day, when Alex was nine, his dad told the family he was going to New York for a short time to try to find some work. He never came home.

"I knew he'd come back as surely as the sun would rise on the Sunshine State," Alex later wrote. "He had been a great dad. He played catch with me. He taught me math. He loved me. But each passing week dug deeper a grave of pain. Finally, my hope dried up and died. I gave up."

❝Playing sports became my dream. I turned into a baseball freak. If I saw a favorite player using a black bat, I'd spend hours using shoe polish and a felt-tip pen to turn mine black too.❞

—ALEX RODRIGUEZ

As painful as it was for young Alex, his mom and siblings rallied around him and showered him with love and affection. To support her children, Lourdes took on two jobs—working in a Miami immigration office during the day and as a waitress at night. While she was at work, Alex's sister, Susy, was the "secretary of education" and helped Alex with his homework, while brother Joe was the "secretary of sports" and coached him on his baseball skills.

The Arteagas also took Alex under their wing. When they'd go to see local baseball games, they'd bring him along. And when Mr. Arteaga bought his son sports equipment, he also purchased some for Alex. "He was the father I didn't have," Alex recalled. "Everything he gave to his son, he gave to me."

Mr. Arteaga took the boys to the Hank Kline Boys & Girls Club in Miami, which had the area's best baseball teams. It was a place where Alex could play his favorite sport and also find a sense of community, something he desperately needed. Instead of staying home after school, he had somewhere to go that made him feel good about himself.

RENAISSANCE MAN

As a boy, Alex admired Leonardo da Vinci, a fifteenth-century artist, scientist, mathematician, and writer. Alex first learned about Leonardo when Lourdes put a print of the *Mona Lisa*, the artist's most famous painting, in his room. Alex liked Leonardo because he was a man of many talents.

At the Boys & Girls Club, Alex met another influential figure in his life, Eddy Rodriguez (no relation to Alex's family), who worked as a coach there. Rodriguez had played minor league baseball. At the club, he had even coached future major leaguers such as Jose Canseco, Rafael Palmeiro, and Alex Fernandez. Alex dreamed of joining those guys in the big leagues one day. "Believe in yourself," Rodriguez told Alex. "But ask more of yourself. This will sustain you in times both good and bad."

Rodriguez's advice had a big effect on young Alex, who was more than willing to put the work in to reach his goals. He focused on his hitting and his fielding, specializing in the shortstop position. He would sometimes sneak into the stadium at the nearby University of Miami so he could learn by watching the college baseball players there.

By then Alex was also a serious student who consistently earned good grades. He later admitted that unlike a lot of kids his age, he liked homework.

When Alex was in sixth grade, he liked a girl so much that he wandered around with his best friend, J.D. Arteaga, for four hours trying to find her house.

His baseball hero was Baltimore Orioles shortstop Cal Ripken Jr. Ripken was six-foot four, bigger than most shortstops but just as agile as smaller players. He was also a great hitter.

But it wasn't only Ripken's skills on the field that impressed Alex. Ripken was also a role model who always signed autographs for his fans. He had such a strong work ethic that he never missed a game. In fact, he went on to set the all-time record for playing the most games in a row—2,632. That's exactly the kind of player Alex wanted to be.

CAL RIPKEN JR.

Cal Ripken Jr., nicknamed the Iron Man, played his first major league baseball game in 1981 for the Baltimore Orioles. He played for the Orioles—first at shortstop, later at third base—for the next twenty years. For much of his career he was coached by his father, Cal Ripken Sr. From 1987 to 1992, Cal's brother Billy Ripken also played for the Orioles. Ripken holds the record for most career home runs by a shortstop, with 345. He also hit 57 homers as a third baseman, bringing his total to 402.

And Alex was doing everything he could to get there. In 1986, when Alex was eleven, his Boys & Girls Club team won the Pony League baseball championship, a national competition for young players. A year later, Alex played shortstop with the club's traveling team, which went to tournaments throughout the southeastern United States. With Alex on board, the squad won two national championships and three city championships. He was even awarded the league batting title one year for having the highest batting average in the league.

Alex was dedicated. While the other boys joked around by the hotel pool after road games, he sat in his room and watched sports news on ESPN, studying the pro players' moves. In the morning, Alex did exercises—one hundred sit-ups and one hundred push-ups. He was also the only player on his team who could hit fastballs.

Alex excelled at more than just baseball. He was also a star basketball player. As a seventh grader, he played on the varsity squad at his school, Kendall Academy. Most of the other players on the team were several years older. Alex also played football, usually holding down the quarterback position, where his quick arm launched fierce touchdown passes.

Although Alex loved baseball, the summer before eighth grade, he felt like he was burning out on the sport. He sat down with his mom and told her how he felt. She didn't want Alex to waste his talent and convinced him to try one more season at the sport.

After Kendall Academy, Alex attended a different school for eighth grade and then went to Christopher Columbus Catholic High School for ninth grade. There he played varsity basketball and baseball. But despite his advanced level of play, Alex wasn't the school's starting shortstop. He served as backup to an older player. His coach told him, "We have a shortstop the next two years. Maybe as a senior you'll get an opportunity to play."

But that wasn't good enough for Alex. He wanted to use the baseball skills he'd worked so hard to hone. His mom agreed that he should find a school where his special athletic gifts wouldn't be wasted. The situation "motivated me to work harder and forced me to look elsewhere," Alex later wrote. The school he found was Westminster Christian High School.

Chapter Two

Field of Dreams

Alex's best friend, J.D. Arteaga, was already attending Westminster, a private school in nearby Fort Lauderdale, Florida. Westminster was known for its strong academic and athletic programs. Alex really wanted to go there, but he faced a major roadblock: his mom couldn't afford the $5,000 yearly tuition. Yet Lourdes felt that Westminster was the right place to help shape Alex as a person, a student, and an athlete. She liked the school's religious classes, tough academics, and emphasis on educating teens to be well-rounded adults. The school seemed like the best spot for her bright, talented son.

Lourdes sat Alex down and told him her plan. If Westminster accepted him for his sophomore year, she would put in more hours of work to make extra money. The family would also apply for financial aid (money from the school) to cover the remaining costs.

At the end of his freshman year at Christopher Columbus Catholic High School, Alex applied to and was accepted at Westminster. He was thrilled. Not only was he joining J.D., he would also be going to a school where many baseball players went on to top-level college teams and the pros. The Westminster Warriors, led by Coach Rich Hofman, were one of the best high school baseball teams in the country. In 1990 the Warriors had won the state baseball championship and had finished tenth in *USA Today*'s national ranking of high school baseball teams.

66*Setbacks and tribulations never stopped Alex from pursuing his dream. It didn't matter what happened around us, he was always focused on his goal.***99**
　　　　　　　　　　　　—LOURDES NAVARRO, ALEX'S MOM

At Westminster, Alex fell easily into campus life. The handsome, green-eyed teen was popular and a good student. "I took school seriously," Alex later wrote. "I made the honor roll and stayed out of trouble, playing all three major sports [baseball, basketball, and football]."

But during football season of his sophomore year, when Alex was fifteen, he experienced a heartbreaking event. Mr. Arteaga was in the stands watching a game when he suffered a heart attack and collapsed. Soon after, he died. "I felt someone had torn my heart out and smashed it," Alex wrote. "J.D. and I grew closer, as brothers. We shared each other's loss, although we really didn't talk about it much. We gave each other strength."

Alex was determined to succeed—and to make Mr. Arteaga proud of him. "I started trying to lead by example and never missed a day of school and always did my homework," Alex remembers.

---

66 *The ripples of his kindness reached many people. He treated me as a son, and I miss him as a father.* 99

—ALEX ON JUAN DIEGO ARTEAGA,
HIS FIRST COACH AND MENTOR

In the spring, Alex hit the baseball field for practice. Coach Hofman didn't exactly see a future MVP when he first met the lean and lanky player. "Alex wasn't Superman. He was a tall, thin, not very strong kid," Hofman recalled. "But he did have real nice actions [on the field]. That helped him defensively, but he was not yet a polished hitter."

Alex had always been a star player before, but he had plenty of competition at Westminster. The squad had many more experienced players. At first Alex wasn't even the team's starting shortstop, but before long he earned the full-time position. He also worked hard on his hitting—and the work paid off.

During the district finals, the team faced off against Gulliver Preparatory School, one of their biggest rivals. In the first inning, Alex came to bat with a runner on base. Omar Fernandez, Gulliver's senior star pitcher, wasn't intimidated by the sophomore batter. He delivered a fastball. As the ball came toward Alex, he swung with all his might. The ball rocketed over the fence in what the *Miami Herald* called "a two-run monster that rainbowed its way over the 375-foot sign in left-center."

Alex's homer helped lead the team to a 10–0 victory against one of their fiercest competitors. Ultimately, though, the Warriors didn't make it to the state championships. It wasn't a star-making season for Alex either—he ended with a .256 batting average (just over 2.5 hits for every 10 at bats—a little more than 25 percent), the lowest average he'd had in his baseball career to that point. But he'd learned a lot and was ready for the next year.

After the season ended, Alex was determined to get stronger. One day Coach Hofman approached him in the weight room. "Well, tenth grade, you had an OK year. Next year everyone will get to know you, and in twelfth grade you'll be the number one pick in the country," Hofman told Alex. Hofman wanted to boost Alex's morale. He thought that if Alex kept working hard, by his senior year, he could be the first high school baseball player chosen by a professional team during the major league draft.

Alex wanted to prove his coach right. Over the summer, he put in grueling sessions at the gym to increase his stamina. He also hit the batting cages to improve his swing.

 In high school, Alex idolized basketball great Michael Jordan.

At age sixteen, when Alex returned to school in the fall of his junior year, he was stronger. He even played quarterback on the Westminster football team. He was picked as an all-state quarterback and led his team to a 9–1 record. College football scouts began showing up at games and calling him one of the best quarterbacks in the state.

By the time Alex arrived for the first practice of the baseball season, Coach Hofman saw a very different player. Alex had shot up two inches and had added thirty pounds of muscle to his frame. He was now six-foot two and weighed 185 pounds. But the extra bulk didn't slow him down. In fact, he was quicker than he had been in his sophomore year, and his reflexes were even keener on the field. "I could bench-press 310 pounds and hit the ball 400 feet," Alex later wrote.

Coach Hofman was impressed with Alex's dedication, and the two formed a special bond. Alex went to the coach for advice and confided in him. Coach Hofman became an important influence on the teenager.

On the field, other teams soon noticed that Alex was a far-improved player. As the season progressed, opposing pitchers became intimidated by his powerful batting. Rather than throw him fastballs, they used slower pitches, such as curveballs, to throw off his timing. Alex was also a fast runner and soon became a talented base stealer.

By the regular season's end, the Warriors had a 32–2 record. They sailed into the state tournament and made it to the finals against Florida Air Academy. With Alex as leadoff batter and J.D. Arteaga as pitcher, the team won the game and became the state AA (small high school) champions. *USA Today* named Westminster the number one high school team in the country, and Alex was one of eight Westminster players named to the all-state team. He also earned all-America honors, awarded to the top high school athletes in the country, with his .477 batting average, 42 stolen bases, 6 home runs, and 52 runs scored.

That summer he was chosen for the USA Baseball Junior National Team and played with the squad in Mexico. Baseball scouts—representatives of pro and college teams who look for young, talented players—saw what Alex was capable of in Mexico. The buzz about him got louder. Baseball scouts look for "five-tool players"—those who can run, throw, field, hit for average (get on base a lot), and hit for power (hit doubles, triples, and home runs). Alex was that kind of player.

Alex began hearing talk about his chances of being recruited to the major leagues, and it made him a little nervous. "I was just a kid, and scouts were talking about what would happen in two or three years. That's an awful lot of pressure to be under," he said.

But he refused to be intimidated. He wanted to focus on reaching his potential as an athlete. His senior-year football season, however, wasn't quite as impressive as his junior year. One day, while tackling during a kickoff, Alex injured his wrist. Everyone—including Alex himself—worried that he had destroyed his chances to play baseball in the spring. The injury turned out to be just a hairline fracture, but it was enough to convince him to give up playing basketball to stay strong for the baseball season.

Alex had always planned on attending college. During his junior year, the University of Miami had awarded him a baseball scholarship. He signed a letter of intent with the university, stating that he planned on enrolling there after high school.

Although he had good friends in school—including J.D.—teenage Alex did little besides homework and sports. During his winter break, instead of relaxing, he played in the Arizona Instructional League, a major league–sponsored program in which young players work on their games alongside older players.

In Arizona being around more experienced players taught Alex about teamwork and made him realize how passionate he was about baseball. For the rest of his senior year, his focus was going to be entirely on the sport.

Chapter Three

Senior Sensation

In 1993, when Alex's senior-year baseball season began, he was in top form. The magazine *Baseball America*, which covers high school and college baseball, named him the number one high school prospect in the country. One college coach described Alex by saying, "If you were to sit in front of a computer and say, 'How would I construct the perfect shortstop?' you'd put all the data in, and then you would see Alex Rodriguez."

That kind of praise made Alex feel good, but it was also a lot of pressure to live up to. And when Alex hit the field for his first game that spring, he could hardly believe his eyes: sitting in the stands were sixty-eight pro and college scouts with notebooks, stopwatches, and radar guns in their hands. They all took notes about Alex. When he ran to first base, they clocked his speed. When he threw the ball, they aimed their radar guns to measure his throws.

After the game, Alex went home and told his mother about all the hoopla. She had sound words of advice for her son: "The scouts are there because they have already seen something they like. So don't change. Just be yourself."

Huge crowds began showing up for Westminster games. Younger kids asked Alex for his autograph. But despite the overwhelming attention, Alex didn't shift his focus from his game. In fact, he kept on improving. In his first ten games of the season, he hit .600, with 7 home runs, 21 RBIs (runs batted in), and 21 steals. At one point, he managed to reach base twenty-one times in a row.

By the season's end, the team had lost only four games. Once again they entered the state tournament. This time they faced Cardinal Newman High School. In the ninth inning, an opposing batter hit a routine ground ball. Alex picked it up but threw too hard, past first base and down the right-field line. Alex's mistake cost the team the game. They were out of the running for the championship.

Luckily Coach Hofman didn't blame Alex for the loss. He understood that even the best players make mistakes from time to time. "Those plays he [usually] does with his eyes closed," said Hofman. "He's meant so much to this team. He's done so much. You can't fault him. He's human."

And Alex certainly didn't suffer much from his error on the field. He finished his season with a .419 average (124 hits in 296 at bats), 17 homers, 70 RBIs, and 90 stolen bases in one hundred games. He was also named the USA Baseball Junior Player of the Year and was a finalist for the Golden Spikes Award, given to the top amateur player in the country. On top of all this, he won the Gatorade National Student-Athlete Award.

The scouts who'd been watching him all season bombarded Alex with offers. Coach Hofman's prediction seemed to be coming true. He was considered the number one draft pick in the United States. Alex didn't know what to do. Should he accept an offer from a major league team or do what he'd always planned on doing—going to college?

BUSY SIGNAL

During his senior year of high school, Alex got thirty to forty calls a night from scouts, college coaches, and sports agents. His sister, Susy, had to come home from college just to help answer all the phone calls.

He needed to talk to someone who'd gone through the same thing. Derek Jeter, who was playing for a New York Yankees minor league team at the time, had been the top high school player a year earlier. Derek had dealt with the same choice Alex had to make. "Everyone in the world was giving me advice—teachers, coaches, friends," Alex recalled. "I decided to call Derek, even though I didn't know him. I figured he knew what I was going through." During the phone call, Derek told Alex to keep his focus on the game and to get professional help in figuring out his future plan.

DEREK JETER

Derek Jeter was born on June 26, 1974, making him one year and one month older than Alex Rodriguez. Derek was born in New Jersey but grew up in Kalamazoo, Michigan. Even as a small child, he was a huge fan of the New York Yankees. In his senior year of high school, the Yankees drafted him and he spent the summer of 1992 with the Gulf Coast League Yankees in Tampa, Florida.

So while Alex weighed his decision, he signed with a sports agent, Scott Boras, who represented big names in baseball such as Barry Bonds and Bernie Williams. As Boras worked behind the scenes to secure a solid professional contract for his new client, Alex also accepted the scholarship from the University of Miami. That way whatever happened, he had options.

When scouts heard that Alex had accepted the college scholarship, they came clamoring even faster, trying to change his mind. Teams faxed offers to Boras's office. The Seattle Mariners had the first draft pick because they had finished last in their division in 1992, so they were most likely to draft Alex. But if Seattle didn't offer Alex a contract, the second pick would go to the Los Angeles Dodgers. Until draft day, it wasn't clear where Alex would end up.

Alex liked the idea of playing in sunny Los Angeles and seeing his family when the Dodgers, part of the National League (NL), played the Florida Marlins in Miami. The Seattle Mariners, on the other hand, were an American League (AL) team and didn't travel to Florida. They also had a long history of losing: their one winning season was in 1991. "The past ten years my teams had won eight championships," Alex later wrote. "All I knew was winning."

On June 3, 1993, the day the draft picks were announced, Alex's pal J.D. hosted a party for him. All of Alex's family and friends were there, anxiously awaiting the news. At 1:14 P.M., the phone rang. It was the Mariners. As expected, they wanted Alex on their team.

But Alex wasn't quick to jump at an offer. When a reporter asked if he was going to sign with the Mariners or go to the University of Miami, Alex answered carefully: "I'm not in a rush.

It depends on how nice [the Mariners] want to be in negotiations. We just want [a deal] that is fair."

THE SEATTLE MARINERS

The Seattle Mariners were established in 1977. The ball club struggled in its early years and did not win more than half its games in a season until 1991, when the Mariners won 83 and lost 79. From 1977 to 1992, the Mariners never made the playoffs.

As his agent began negotiating with the Mariners, Alex was named *USA Today*'s national high school player of the year. He also got to participate in the Olympic Festival, run by the U.S. Olympic Committee, which prepares young athletes for international competition. During the festival, Alex traveled to a tournament in San Antonio, Texas. At a game in July, while Alex was in the dugout, a wildly thrown warm-up ball hit him in the side of the face and knocked him out. His cheekbone was broken—but he would be okay.

As Alex healed, negotiations continued between Alex's agent and the Mariners. Boras wanted at least $1 million per year for his client, but the Mariners offered less. University of

Miami classes were scheduled to start in late August. According to the rules of professional baseball, if Alex attended classes there, the Mariners would lose their draft rights, and he'd be ineligible for professional play for the next three years.

With the Mariners deal stalled, on August 31, Alex decided to go to school. As he walked through the campus, a scout from the Mariners stopped him before he could go inside one of the buildings. The team was willing to keep negotiating. By 2:00 A.M., Alex and the Mariners had agreed on a record-setting $1.35-million contract.

Soon Alex was sitting at his mother's kitchen table, along with members of the Mariners front office, and signing his name to the contract. What he had dreamed about his entire life had come true. He was going to play professional baseball.

Chapter Four

The Go-Between

After Alex signed with the Mariners in the summer of 1993, the eighteen-year-old player asked to talk to Chuck Armstrong, the team's president, in private. He wanted to make sure that all the tough negotiating hadn't put a damper on their relationship. And Alex wanted Armstrong to know that he was ready, in mind and body, to be the best player possible.

Alex had suddenly become a millionaire. But he didn't want to get carried away with foolish purchases. With his agent's help, he set up a budget plan. From his paycheck, he would take $500 in cash and a $500 credit card allowance every month. The rest would go into the bank. Alex allowed himself a few special purchases, though, including a black-and-gold Jeep for himself and a Mercedes-Benz for his mother. Best of all, he paid off the mortgage (money owed) on his mother's house. With this gift, he wanted to thank her for all she'd done for him.

In early September, Alex traveled to Seattle to visit the team and tour the city. His tour guide was Ken Griffey Jr., a twenty-three-year-old batting champion and one of Seattle's most popular players. The two young men instantly hit it off. Griffey understood what Alex had gone through during the drafting process. Griffey had been the first draft pick in 1987 and knew what that kind of pressure was like.

To prepare for the spring season, Alex traveled to Peoria, Arizona. He lived in a dormitory and trained once again with the Arizona Instructional League. Team manager John McNamara quickly got a strong impression of Alex's talent. In his first game, Alex kept five batters from scoring with his lightning-quick fielding. "You couldn't ask for a better-played game of shortstop," McNamara said. "The kid looks and plays mature. He's loaded with talent, all the tools they've been talking about."

---

66 *[Alex is] a down-to-earth guy. He works his butt off just like everybody else.*99

—FORMER SEATTLE MARINER ANDY SHEETS

Equally important, Alex got along well with his teammates. When a sporting goods company sent him a huge supply of equipment, he shared it with the other guys.

Following his time in Arizona, Alex headed home to Miami for several months. He wanted to keep up his fitness level. He spent five hours a day lifting weights, running, and fielding.

Before he knew it, it was late February and time for spring training. Saying good-bye was tough on his mother, Lourdes, who drove her teenage son to the airport. "I wanted to cry," she later said, "but I could not allow myself to do that. I couldn't let him see that I was worried or sad or even scared for him. I was the tree trunk of the family, and the tree trunk cannot fall or else all the branches will go with it."

❝ You get vibes from young players. The kid who is scared sits at the end of the bench. This spring, when I was ready to [bring young players off the bench], Alex always became highly visible. He would grab a bat or his glove. In his own way, he was telling me he was ready. ❞

—FORMER SEATTLE MARINERS MANAGER LOU PINIELLA

When Alex arrived at the Mariners' spring training camp in Arizona, he was amazed at the dedication of the other major leaguers. Practice began at 10:00 A.M., but one day, Alex arrived at 7:00 A.M. and a few other players were already there. Training ended at 2:00 P.M. But once Alex forgot his pager and returned at 6:00 P.M. to find batting champ Edgar Martinez practicing his swing in the batting cages. "Those veterans showed me that success in anything begins with dedication and hard work," Alex later wrote.

When spring training was over, the team sent Alex to Appleton, Wisconsin, where he would be playing for the Mariners' Class A minor league team, the Appleton Foxes of the Midwest League. (The minor leagues are divided into several classes: rookie league is the lowest, followed by Class A, Class AA, and Class AAA.) In Appleton, Alex shared an apartment with a married player and his wife.

During his first week of the season, Alex slammed his first professional home run against the Springfield Sultans. The hit was one of his longest ever—440 feet. He learned a valuable lesson as he dropped his bat and casually jogged around the bases after the home run. The other team's manager accused Alex of trying to embarrass the pitcher. Alex didn't realize that in pro ball, it's considered bad form to take your time running around the bases.

Several weeks into the season, Alex was hitting only .280, lower than his potential. Frustrated, he called his mother and told her he wanted to come home. In response, she told him to go out and play harder. Alex realized he was giving up too easily—he just had to tough it out. He was glad he did. A few more weeks passed, and he increased his average to above .300.

After sixty-five games with Appleton, he had hit .319, with 14 home runs and 55 RBIs. He was chosen to play in the Midwest League's all-star game, but at that point, he had already been promoted to the next minor league level, the Class AA Jacksonville Suns in the Southern League. During his first game with the team, he scored a home run.

Then three weeks later, he was promoted all the way up to the major leagues to join the Mariners for a game in Boston. Alex couldn't believe it. "I stayed up late calling family, friends, and old coaches—'I'm going to the show!'" he told them.

BIG-LEAGUE TEASING

At his first major league game with the Mariners, a teammate handed Alex coupons to a fast-food restaurant and joked, "You're making one point three million. When you get sent back down to the minors, take the guys out to lunch down there."

At only eighteen, he was the youngest major league player in ten years (Jose Rijo had become a New York Yankee at age nineteen in 1984). Although some members of the Mariners staff thought it was too soon to bring Alex on board, the team's manager, Lou Piniella, fought to bring him there. Piniella felt the Mariners "needed a spark," and he hoped Alex would provide that spark.

On July 8, 1994, Alex started at shortstop against the Boston Red Sox. As Alex headed to the plate for his first at bat, he was incredibly nervous. "My body felt jittery, and my knees buckled. I could barely stand," he later wrote.

Although he went hitless in all three of his tries at bat, his fielding was solid. The following night, he had two hits. After seventeen games, Alex was hitting .204. But by August, a more serious problem put an end to Alex's time in the major leagues. The contract between the major league players and team owners had expired, and the two sides couldn't reach an agreement. The owners shut down the major league season on August 11. The minor league baseball season, however, was still in full swing.

The Mariners didn't want Alex sitting around during the strike—he needed to keep getting experience. So on August 2, management sent him to the Mariners' Class AAA team in Calgary, Canada, where he ended the season. It was a good choice. The remainder of the major league season, including the World Series, was canceled that year. Alex looked at his time in Calgary as an opportunity to improve his skills further. When his season there ended, he walked away with a respectable .311 average, 6 home runs, and 21 RBIs.

Instead of going home to Miami, he decided to play in a winter league in the Dominican Republic. Many players from the minor and major leagues go to the challenging winter leagues to keep their skills in tip-top shape.

It was Alex's first time back to the island since he was a little boy. But it proved to be a tough experience. Alex garnered only a .179 batting average and wasn't up to par against his tough competition. "I was overmatched and my mind really wasn't into it," Alex later admitted. "I think [the league] woke me up a little bit. I recommend it to every young player."

THE NEW GUY

Alex experienced some good-natured hazing as a rookie. After one game, his Mariners teammates stole his clothes while he was showering. "When I got out of the shower, all my clothes were gone," he recalled. "Instead, [my teammates made me] sign thirty autographs while wearing a silver dress and balancing in high-heeled shoes."

Back in the United States in February, the baseball strike was still in effect. Alex worked out in the Mariners' minor league camp with the Class AAA team, which had by then moved from Calgary to Tacoma, Washington.

In April, Alex started the 1995 season with the minor league Tacoma Rainiers. But on May 6, he was called up to the major leagues again after another player was injured. He struggled at bat and on May 27 was sent back to Tacoma. Then ten days later, with more Mariners injuries, he returned to the majors.

On June 12, during a game against the Kansas City Royals, Alex scored his first major league home run. It was an unbelievable feeling. Later in the game, he made an impressive defensive play. Although the Mariners lost the game 10–9, Alex still felt good about his role.

Yet three weeks later, he was back in Tacoma and working on hitting curveballs, one of his few weaknesses. He soon returned to the Mariners, only to be sent back down one more time. "I became a human yo-yo going between Tacoma and Seattle," Alex wrote.

Being sent down to the minors was eating away at his self-confidence. He didn't know what to do. Alex even considered going back home and attending the University of Miami, where his best friend, J.D. Arteaga, was playing on the college team. But as always, his mom told him to keep working hard. "I'm so thankful Mom talked me out of it," he wrote. "I know now the adversity made me stronger."

Finally all his back-and-forth shuttling came to an end. On August 31, Alex was brought up to play with the Mariners for the rest of the 1995 season. Although he was only a backup shortstop to Luis Sojo, the twenty-year-old player was thrilled to be part of the excitement. The team made its way to the play-offs for the first time ever and beat the Yankees three games to two in the American League Division Series. "It was an awesome experience," Alex told *Sports Illustrated*.

THE POSTSEASON

After the 162-game regular season ends, four teams from the National League and four teams from the American League take part in the postseason playoffs. The teams are the winners of the three divisions in each league (Central, East, and West), along with a wildcard team from each league. The wildcard team is the team with the next-best season record after the division winners.

The first round of playoff games is a best-of-five series (the first team to win three games wins). The winners then play a best-of-seven series (the first team to win four games wins) for the league championship. After this series, there are two teams left—the American League champs and the National League champs. They play each other in a best-of-seven series—the World Series.

Unfortunately, when the Mariners went up against the Cleveland Indians in the American League Championship

Series, they lost four games to two. After the final game, the home fans at the Seattle Kingdome gave their team—whose motto was "Refuse to Lose"—a "thunderous, moving ovation . . . to show their thanks for the season's incredible ride that saved baseball in Seattle," Alex recalled. The exciting postseason gave Seattle fans something to cheer about and a renewed interest in their home team.

Alex's up-and-down 1995 season gave him a lot to think about. More than anything, it made him want to work hard to be a permanent member of the Mariners. He was determined never to return to the minors.

Chapter Five

Hitting the Big Time

In the off-season, Alex went home to Miami to spend time with his family and friends. He also used his time off to study the batting patterns of a real champ. He watched tapes of Mariners teammate Edgar Martinez, who had led the American League in hitting in 1995 with a .358 average.

"The tapes were three hours long, all his hits from [1994] and [1995]," Alex later said. "I watched them about three times a week. . . . If you have a great hitter, if you have a great player, why not take the opportunities to look at them and do some of the great things they do?"

He also worked with a personal trainer to get in top physical shape. So when Alex arrived at spring training in the winter of 1996, he was ready for action. He walked up to team manager Lou Piniella and confidently said, "I'm ready." Piniella replied, "I know you are."

His teammates quickly noticed that Alex was no longer playing like a rookie. He was more self-assured at the plate and in his fielding. The Mariners traded shortstop Luis Sojo to the Yankees that year, and Alex was promoted to be the Mariners' new starting shortstop.

But Alex's first few games weren't exactly awe inspiring. In his first nineteen at bats, he got only two hits. But then, during an April 9 game in Detroit's Tiger Stadium, he hit a 440-foot home run. Within two weeks, he was hitting .375. In an April 21 game against the Toronto Blue Jays, however, Alex pulled a hamstring, a muscle in his leg. The injury put him out of commission for several weeks.

During the 1996 season, Alex told a reporter that he hadn't gone to his own prom. So, thousands of Seattle-area girls bombarded him with invitations to go to their proms.

When he had healed, Alex returned to the game refreshed and charged. Piniella saw the fire in him and moved him up in the batting order from ninth to the number-two spot, right in front of Ken Griffey Jr. That boost of confidence from Piniella meant a lot to Alex. He was going to run with it. Soon the one-two punch of Rodriguez and Griffey was a dangerous combination.

On May 12, Alex had his first two-homer game against Kansas City. Five days later, he hit a grand slam (a homer with runners on all the bases). By June 25, he had hit 15 home runs. His batting average for June was .324. And things just kept getting better.

Alex quickly became the team heartthrob. Girls squealed when they saw him. Fans cheered his name. Attendance at home games went up by more than ten thousand per game because everyone wanted a glimpse of the rising superstar. And soon fans gave Alex his own nickname: A-Rod. But he didn't want to get distracted from what was most important: his game.

From June 19 to July 6, A-Rod hit in sixteen of seventeen games. His average rose to .341, which made him sixth in the league standings. And he wasn't even twenty-one years old. He was selected to play on the American League All-Star team, the youngest shortstop ever to play in an All-Star game. Unfortunately, the National League won the game.

When he returned from the All-Star matchup, A-Rod continued to heat up home plate. Teammate Ken Griffey Jr. had nothing but praise for him. "He works hard, he's a smart kid, I think he's in the right situation," Griffey told *Sports Illustrated*. "Everyone knows he's going to be a special player."

THEY'RE ALL-STARS!

In July—at the midpoint of the regular pro baseball season—Major League Baseball holds the All-Star game. The game pits the best players from the American League against the best players from the National League. Fans vote to determine which players will take part in the game. Managers choose the pitchers.

The All-Star game is an exhibition game. For many years, winning or losing didn't really matter. But as of 2003, the league that wins the All-Star game gets home-field advantage during the World Series—so winning the All-Star game has become more important.

The Mariners front office was delighted with A-Rod's performance and wanted to show it. On July 25, 1996, two days before his birthday, the Mariners tore up his old contract and replaced it with a new one: he would earn $10.6 million over four years. A-Rod was speechless. The season before, he had been commuting between the minors and the majors. This season he had carved out a place for himself alongside the big boys.

In August A-Rod's stats went through the roof. He hit .435 and was named Player of the Month, only the sixth time a Mariner had been given that honor. Then he won the American

League's batting crown by having the highest average in the league. He'd hit in fifty-two of his last sixty games and finished the season with a .358 average. A-Rod was the third-youngest batting crown winner in AL history (after Ty Cobb and Al Kaline), and he was the first shortstop to receive the title in more than fifty years. He had 215 hits in the season, more than any other shortstop in history. On top of all of this, he had 36 homers, 3 grand slams, 123 RBIs, and a league-leading 54 doubles and 379 total bases. On the field, he was just as impressive. He'd committed just 15 errors in 657 fielding chances.

But even though the Mariners won eighty-five games, they finished in second place in the American League West, four games behind the Texas Rangers. They were out of the running for the postseason.

66*Although being a millionaire at age eighteen changed my material value, it hasn't changed my personal values. It's not how much you make that counts. It's what you do with it.*99

—Alex Rodriguez

Despite that disappointment, the individual honors for A-Rod kept streaming in. The Associated Press and *Sporting News* named him Player of the Year. He didn't win the league's

Most Valuable Player award (two baseball writers from each team's city vote on the MVP), but he was just three votes behind the Texas Rangers' Juan Gonzalez for the honor.

High praise came from his childhood idol, Cal Ripken Jr. "All that Alex seems to need is experience to become the short-stop everyone else will be watching in our league," Ripken said. "The future belongs to Alex Rodriguez."

A-Rod played another role off the field. As a Latino—a person of Latin American heritage—he was a role model for young Latino boys and girls. A-Rod took this job very seriously. "I'm proud to be an American and proud that my parents are Dominican," he said.

A-Rod used his newfound fame to do positive things. He was always willing to meet and greet fans and sign autographs. He visited Seattle-area grade schools and encouraged students to focus on reading, math, physical fitness, and good citizenship. He'd say things like, "Math is very important, to keep up with Ken Griffey's batting average." Learning had always been important to A-Rod, and he wanted to instill that love in his young fans.

When A-Rod returned home to Florida after the season, he went back to the place that had nurtured his love for baseball—the Hank Kline Boys & Girls Club. He visited his pal and former coach Eddy Rodriguez and gave him some happy news: A-Rod was donating $25,000 to build a new baseball field behind the club. "No other player has ever come back to this place and given like Alex has," Rodriguez said. "Alex just did it. 'Whatever you need,' he said."

A-Rod also bought a new house for himself, just a few blocks from his mother's home in Kendall. He played golf with pal Derek Jeter, who had become a close friend since they first spoke during the younger player's senior year of high school. He also decided to buy a home in Seattle, since he was settled in with the Mariners.

WALL OF HONOR

A-Rod was such a fan of Baltimore Orioles star shortstop Cal Ripken Jr. that when he moved into his own home, he took an old poster of Ripken from his childhood days, framed it, and put it up in his new house.

Then an offer came along that A-Rod couldn't resist. He was asked to go to Japan with a team of star major leaguers to play a series of exhibition games (games played just for show). Cal Ripken Jr. was a member of the team. During their time in Japan, A-Rod got to know his hero. "We spent time together every day. I learned so much, not just about baseball, but about life," A-Rod said. "What I learned from Cal is to respect the game, respect the fans. Nothing fancy out there. Just do your job."

At the start of the 1997 season, that's exactly what twenty-one-year-old A-Rod did. By mid-April he was batting .333. During a hot hitting streak beginning in June, A-Rod achieved a memorable feat. In a June 5 game against the Detroit Tigers, he hit for the cycle, which means he hit a single, a double, a triple, and a home run in the same game. He was only the second Mariner ever to accomplish this feat (Jay Buhner had been the first).

But a few days later, A-Rod collided with Toronto Blue Jays pitcher Roger Clemens. He had to sit out two weeks with a rib injury. When he returned on June 27, he was feeling strong and ready for whatever the game would throw at him. In his first at bat, he hit a home run against the Anaheim Angels' Chuck Finley.

A-Rod's teammates were also doing well. Pitcher Randy Johnson, who had been injured during the 1996 season, was helping lead the team to victory. Edgar Martinez, whose batting style A-Rod had once studied, was one of the league's leading hitters. And Ken Griffey Jr. had hit 30 home runs by the All-Star break (midway through the season). Meanwhile, once again A-Rod was picked to be the starting shortstop at the All-Star game.

After the All-Star break, A-Rod and his teammates were playing spectacularly. They won the American League West title and then faced the Baltimore Orioles—Cal Ripken's team—in the playoffs. Unfortunately, they lost in the first round to the Orioles, three games to one. That was the end of their postseason.

Although 1997 hadn't been as good as 1996, A-Rod was still proud of his stats. He had batted .300 and had 23 home runs and 84 RBIs.

"*Alex's composure and maturity level are impressive. A lot of players come in with raw talent, but they don't know how to play or handle themselves off the field. Alex does both well.***"**

—CAL RIPKEN JR.

When the 1997 season wrapped up, A-Rod wanted to stay out of the limelight as much as he could. He worked on writing a children's book, *Alex Rodriguez: Hit a Grand Slam!*, with the help of sportswriter Greg Brown. And in January, he took a college class. "My continuing education is so important to me that I took my first college courses," he wrote. "I'm determined to get a college degree someday. I don't care if it takes me ten years."

A-Rod also went back to the Boys & Girls Club to work out with coach Eddy Rodriguez. There he received a special honor. A new baseball field for which he'd donated money was named the Alex Rodriguez Baseball Field. "I'm really proud of that,"

A-Rod said. "It's got a bronze statue of me out in front and my picture on a wall."

The tribute was to A-Rod's generosity and talent. He wanted to live up to his reputation for greatness. He planned on doing just that in the next season.

Chapter Six

Seeing 40-40

A-Rod continued his work with young people during the winter of 1997. He put on baseball clinics to teach elementary-school-age baseball players the basics of the game. He also wanted to nurture a young person on a more personal level. Before the start of the 1998 season, he decided to help out an underprivileged Miami boy and show him a better way of life. A-Rod took him to charity functions and even let the boy stay at his house when he wasn't there.

But one day, after A-Rod returned from a trip, he found his home vandalized, his expensive suits stolen, and more than $100,000 in cash missing. Even his All-Star game jersey, with Cal Ripken's signature on it, was gone. The thief was the young man A-Rod had tried to help. "I felt violated. . . . There is no other way to describe it," A-Rod told reporters. He had trusted someone who had taken terrible advantage of him. From then on, Alex was going to be a lot more careful about how and whom he helped. It was a valuable lesson for the trusting young player.

❝Speaking at schools has shown me that sometimes encouragement is the best gift, and that doesn't cost anything.❞

—ALEX RODRIGUEZ

Despite the disappointment, A-Rod wanted to keep his focus on the field. When he returned for the 1998 season, his eye was on having a winning season. As April progressed, he was batting great numbers. In three games from April 18 to April 20, he tied a seventy-one-year-old American League record with eight extra-base hits—four doubles, two triples, and two home runs. During a May 16 game against the Toronto Blue Jays, Alex swatted in two homers and four RBIs. In June he batted .328 for the month and was chosen as the American League's starting shortstop for the All-Star game, where he knocked out a homer and helped the AL win 13–8.

Home runs were becoming the norm for A-Rod. In mid-July he slammed balls out of the park in three straight games, and on July 19, he hit his 30th round-tripper of the season. Two weeks later, he stole his 29th and 30th bases of the year in a game against the Yankees. There to congratulate him on joining the 30-30 Club (30 home runs and 30 stolen bases in a season) was pal Derek Jeter, the Yanks' shortstop.

That momentum kept A-Rod going at a lightning pace. In July and August, he hit in twelve straight games, and on August 12, he hit his 36th homer of the season. For the month of August, he batted .347.

While he was having an astounding season, some of his Mariners teammates weren't having a great time. Star pitcher Randy Johnson, the anchor of the Mariners pitching staff, asked to be traded because he wasn't happy with the team's overall record. He was sent to the Houston Astros. In his place, a crop of young pitchers came on board.

The team as a whole wasn't performing exceptionally. By the end of August, the Mariners were in last place in the AL West with a 61–71 record.

But A-Rod wasn't going to give up on the rest of the season. On September 8, he hit his 39th home run of the year, and two days later he stole his 41st base. Then on September 19, he hit a home run in the first inning against Anaheim Angels pitcher Jack McDowell. He was now an official member—the third ever—of the 40-40 Club (40 homers and 40 stolen bases).

Three days later, A-Rod hit his 41st homer against the Oakland Athletics, breaking the American League record for homers by a shortstop (Rico Petrocelli had hit 40 in 1969). By season's end, A-Rod had hit his 42nd.

JOIN THE CLUB

In 1988 Jose Canseco, a right fielder with the Oakland Athletics, became the first ballplayer to hit 40 home runs and steal 40 bases in a single season. He was twenty-four years old. Barry Bonds of the San Francisco Giants became the second member of that club in 1996 at age thirty-two. A-Rod was just twenty-three years old when he joined the club in 1998. Coincidentally, all three ballplayers celebrate birthdays in the month of July.

During the 1998 season, A-Rod played in every game, batted .310, and led the league with 213 hits, 686 at bats, and 64 multi-hit games. He also stole 46 bases and made only 18 errors on the field. The Mariners ultimately ended up in third place in the AL West with a 76–85 record.

With the season ending, A-Rod returned to his charity work. He created the Alex Rodriguez Foundation, a children's charity. And along with military and political leader Colin Powell and actor Denzel Washington, he became a spokesperson for the Boys & Girls Clubs of America. Around this time,

A-Rod also began dating Cynthia Scurtis, a Miami high school psychology teacher. Things were coming into place in his life.

The ballplayer felt clearheaded and ready for the 1999 season. But two games in, A-Rod twisted his left knee and tore some cartilage. He had to undergo surgery, and he missed thirty-two games.

During this time, many people questioned whether the star shortstop would stick with the Mariners. A-Rod was honest about the fact that he wanted to go to the World Series. On a Web site devoted to A-Rod, he wrote about talking with Mariners management about putting together a championship team with solid players.

❝I want to be known as a good major leaguer, and good major leaguers work to become good.**❞**

—ALEX RODRIGUEZ

With A-Rod sidelined, the Mariners fell into a slump. They were 15–20 before he returned to the fold in a May 21 game against the Kansas City Royals. With his knee healed, A-Rod was back in fine form, and at his first at bat, he homered. Then he helped lead his team to a six-game winning streak, during which he hit .304 with three homers.

After losing the next two games, the Mariners bounced back and were victorious in four games. Their record jumped back over .500 (more wins than losses) to 25–24.

A-Rod then went on a thirteen-game hitting streak, raising his average to .357. And during a game against the Orioles, he stole the 100th base of his career. But in August, after hitting his 34th and 35th home runs of the year in a game against the Chicago White Sox, he went into a slump. He batted .104 over the next month, and his season average fell to .287. He turned things around on September 16 when he hit a grand slam in the eighth inning against Tampa Bay.

Go the Distance

In 1999 Seattle Mariners fans were thrilled when the old Kingdome was replaced by the new Safeco Field. But the new stadium gave A-Rod and his teammates a challenge. Since the new stadium was much bigger than the old dome, it was more difficult to hit home runs there.

Unfortunately, once again the Mariners weren't going to the postseason. For the second year in a row, they finished third in the American League West, this time with a 79–83 record.

One of the bright spots of the season was that the team had a new home stadium, the open-air Safeco Field, which replaced the smaller, enclosed Kingdome.

Ultimately A-Rod ended the 1999 season with a .285 average. But he had driven in 111 runs, knocked in 42 homers, stolen 21 bases, and hit 25 doubles. Despite his overall good season, much of the attention that year was focused on the home-run race between Mark McGwire, Sammy Sosa, and A-Rod's teammate Ken Griffey Jr.

MARK McGWIRE

Mark McGwire made quite an impression in 1987, his rookie year. Playing for the Oakland Athletics, he set a record for most home runs by a rookie, with 49. The six-foot five first baseman was known as a power hitter throughout his career. In 1997 McGwire was traded to the St. Louis Cardinals midseason. The following year he slammed 70 home runs, setting a new record for home runs in a single season. The previous record holder was Roger Maris, a member of the New York Yankees who hit 61 homers in 1961.

Even though Alex wasn't the center of attention, people were still taking notice of him. "He's a complete player," said

Rudy Terrasas, a scout for the Texas Rangers. "He can beat you in all facets of the game—with his power, his speed, and his glove. And he's still young, with a tremendous upside. People who play like he does are usually twenty-eight, twenty-nine, thirty years old. He's not even twenty-four and doing it. For my money, if I was starting a club and needed a shortstop . . . he'd be my choice." With the 2000 season ahead of him, A-Rod was going to have some interesting choices to make.

Chapter Seven

Making History

With the close of the 1999 season, questions were flying about whether A-Rod would re-sign with the Mariners. His contract was going to expire after the 2000 season, and he would be a free agent, able to choose whatever team he'd like to play for next.

In October 1999, Mariners chairman Howard Lincoln told the media that he'd make offers to both A-Rod and Ken Griffey Jr. that would make them the highest-paid players in baseball. Griffey told A-Rod to keep his mind on his game, not on the contract negotiations. But A-Rod couldn't help but think about them. "I've never been under such a microscope," he said in an interview with the *Sporting News*. "I'm not experienced with this. It's not like fielding a ground ball or hitting the curve."

Before the 2000 season began, Griffey decided it was time to make a move. He requested a trade to the Cincinnati Reds.

Alex Rodriguez attended Westminster Christian High School, where he had a .505 batting average his senior year. He graduated in 1993, and the school named him to its baseball Hall of Fame.

Alex's biggest fan has always been his mom, Lourdes. This photo is from 1997, his fourth year with the Seattle Mariners.

Outfielder Ken Griffey Jr. was Alex's first friend on the Seattle Mariners. Here, they high-five each other during a 1999 game against the San Diego Padres. The Mariners won 9–1.

While playing for the Mariners, Alex was given the nickname A-Rod. He quickly gained a reputation as a stellar shortstop, playing in his first All-Star game in 1996, his first full year in the major leagues.

In 2001 A-Rod left Seattle to join the Texas Rangers. His ten-year, $252-million contract with the Rangers made him the highest-paid athlete in the history of professional sports.

A-Rod played with the Rangers for only three years, but he was hugely popular with fans.

Alex helps unload a truckload of computers in Chicago, Illinois. In 2003 he pledged to donate one computer to the Boys & Girls Clubs each time he recorded a run batted in (RBI). He finished the year with 118 RBIs.

In 2004 the Rangers traded A-Rod to the New York Yankees. His good friend Derek Jeter *(right)* was the team's shortstop, so Alex *(left)* switched to play third base. His uniform number also changed from number 3 to number 13.

Alex married Miami schoolteacher Cynthia Scurtis after the end of the 2002 baseball season. After Alex finished his first season with the Yankees, Cynthia gave birth to their daughter, Natasha Alexander Rodriguez.

A-Rod hit his 400th career home run on June 8, 2005, in a game against the Milwaukee Brewers. He's the youngest player in major league history to reach that historic mark.

The trade was a big deal for A-Rod, who'd always looked up to Griffey, the first person he became friends with when he joined the Mariners. There had been some rivalry between the two star players over the years, yet they also had a special connection. "It's like a big brother-little brother relationship," explained Griffey.

KEN GRIFFEY JR.

Ken Griffey Jr. grew up in Cincinnati, Ohio, where he learned to play baseball from a major leaguer—his father, Ken Griffey Sr. Griffey Sr. played outfield for the Cincinnati Reds from 1973 to 1981. The Seattle Mariners drafted Griffey Jr. in 1987, and in 1990 and 1991, father and son played together for the Mariners. Griffey Jr. is known for his great home-run production and his outstanding abilities in center field.

With Griffey gone, A-Rod was the team's only big star and was generally considered the Mariners' new leader. But with pitcher Randy Johnson also traded, what would the Mariners' 2000 season be like? Would they have a shot?

To many people's surprise, the Mariners had a strong season. With powerhouse pitchers Aaron Sele and Kazuhiro Sasaki and first baseman John Olerud on board, they had shored up their lineup. As they moved toward the postseason, it was clear that this time, they had a shot at going to the playoffs. "We're having a blast," said A-Rod.

A-Rod was becoming a team leader. His calm strength inspired his teammates, especially the younger ones, who looked up to him. He was a force at the plate and on the field.

As the last day of the season approached, the Mariners played the Oakland Athletics (also known as the Oakland A's) for the division title. And even though the A's beat Seattle, the Mariners weren't out of the running for the postseason. Because they had the best record of the teams that didn't win their divisions, the Mariners qualified for the postseason wild-card spot.

In the first round of the playoffs—the American League Division Series (ALDS)—Seattle faced the Chicago White Sox. The Mariners knew it would be key to have strong pitching and keep White Sox slugger Frank Thomas from scoring. Game one took place in Chicago's Comiskey Park. For nine innings, the game was close; the teams were tied 4–4 at the end of the ninth. In the top of the tenth, Edgar Martinez hit a two-run home run and John Olerud followed that up with a solo homer. Chicago didn't manage to score at all in the bottom of the inning, giving the Mariners a 7–4 victory.

The Mariners needed only nine innings to win game two 5–2. Then they headed back to Safeco Field, where they planned to finish off the series in front of a hometown crowd. Game three was close, but Seattle pulled off a 2–1 win. They were one step closer to the World Series!

The Mariners were up against the New York Yankees in their quest for the American League pennant, or championship. The team that won the American League Championship Series (ALCS) would go to the World Series. On paper, the Mariners looked good. They had a 91–71 regular-season record, compared with New York's 87–74 record. But New York had a lot of playoff experience and had won the World Series in 1998 and 1999.

Finally the Mariners were on their way to the big time, and A-Rod was happy. But this would be a tough fight. The Yankees were the world champions. A-Rod was going to have to step up his game for the Mariners to have a shot against New York.

66*He's Mr. Clean. He's milk and cookies.*99
—FORMER SEATTLE MARINER DAVID SEGUI, REMARKING ON A-ROD'S NICE-GUY IMAGE

In the first matchup, Mariners pitcher Freddy Garcia's fiery arm kept the Yanks from scoring any runs. The Mariners took a

1–0 lead into the sixth inning. Then A-Rod came to bat with no one on base against Yankees pitcher Denny Neagle. He hit a foul ball on a 3–1 count (three balls, one strike), making the count 3–2. On the next pitch, Neagle threw A-Rod a fastball. That was just what Alex needed. He powered a home run to left field. Seattle took a 2–0 lead and won the game.

There was electricity in the air. Could the Mariners beat the Yanks again?

In game two, the Mariners took an early lead, but the Yankees seemed determined to crush the Mariners' World Series hopes. A-Rod's pal Derek Jeter hit a two-run homer in the eighth inning to help his team to a 7–1 victory.

The series moved to Seattle for the next three games. But the Yankees continued to dominate, winning game three 8–2 and game four 5–0. One more win would give the Yankees the pennant. The Mariners played hard in game five, and they pulled off a 6–2 win. Alex batted in two runs in the fifth inning to contribute to the win.

Game six took place back at Yankee Stadium. Even after New York was leading 9–4 in the seventh inning, Seattle didn't give up. A-Rod started off the eighth inning with a home run, and the Mariners followed up with two more runs, but that was all they could manage. The final score was New York 9, Seattle 7. The Mariners' promising season had come to a disappointing end.

Overall A-Rod had had a great season, hitting .316 and 41 homers, scoring a career-best 132 RBIs, earning 34 doubles and 134 runs, drawing 100 walks, and committing only 10 errors. In the ALCS, he had a stellar .409 batting average. When asked if he planned on staying with the Mariners for another season, A-Rod answered carefully. "I absolutely see scenarios where I'm in Seattle next year," he said. "But at the same time, I see scenarios where I'm elsewhere."

❝If they go out and get the pieces [championship-level players], sure, I'd be more than willing to sign with the Mariners.**❞**

—ALEX RODRIGUEZ, ON WHETHER
HE WOULD RE-SIGN WITH SEATTLE

It was a confusing time for Alex. He felt a certain loyalty to the Mariners, who'd given him his major league start when he was only eighteen years old. But A-Rod was frustrated with his team for not taking it to the limit. He wasn't in the game to just have a great season personally. He wanted to be part of a winning team.

A-Rod was a huge prospect for other teams. By then he was on the free-agent market, and ball clubs were vying for him. Everybody wanted a piece of Alex Rodriguez. Wherever he went in Seattle, whether it was his favorite restaurant or the clubhouse, scouts would follow. He was on everyone's hit list.

Many thought that if he left the Mariners, he would go to the New York Mets or the Los Angeles Dodgers, the team he had wanted to join when he was in high school. But these teams didn't pursue him. A-Rod's agent, Scott Boras, was asking for a $200-million contract. For some teams, A-Rod was too expensive. The Atlanta Braves and the New York Yankees passed on him, and eventually the Mariners decided not to bid for him anymore. But many other teams were still chasing him. It became a favorite game among sportswriters to guess which team A-Rod would sign with.

In December, A-Rod would have to make a decision. Everybody's eyes were on him. What would he do? By then the Chicago White Sox and the Texas Rangers were the only two teams willing to pay the $200-million asking price.

After weeks of negotiations, on December 11, 2000, A-Rod signed an astonishing $252-million contract, to be paid out over ten years, with the Texas Rangers (based near Dallas in Arlington, Texas). The contract made A-Rod the highest-paid athlete in the history of professional sports.

A-Rod's contract included a no-trade clause (which meant he couldn't be traded without his approval) plus an escape clause that granted him the right to become a free agent after seven years. The Rangers also agreed to up his pay if another player signed for more money than he made. For example, if another player signed a contract for $300 million, A-Rod's salary would go up to $301 million, and he would remain the highest-paid player in baseball.

If there's a player deserving of the largest contract in baseball, it's this player.

—TOM HICKS, OWNER OF THE TEXAS RANGERS

A-Rod had always said he wanted to play for a winning team, so it came as a surprise to some people that he signed with the Rangers. The Rangers lost ninety-one games in 2000 and had won only one postseason contest since the team had formed in 1972. Yet A-Rod saw an opportunity to make the Rangers a victorious squad. He also wanted to work hard and prove that he was worth the big money he was earning.

It was an exciting but crazy time for A-Rod. Everyone wanted to talk to—and write about—this 252-million-dollar man. Everyone from gum manufacturers to vacuum cleaner and car companies wanted to pay him to be a spokesperson. A slew of endorsement offers came his way.

It was time for him to get some peace. He sold his home in Seattle and returned home to Miami, where he could spend time with his mom, his girlfriend, and his friends. He would need all the support he could get. A-Rod had a big year—and a lot of changes—ahead of him.

Chapter Eight

Most Valuable Player

A-Rod enjoyed his time home in Miami over the holiday season. He hung out with Cynthia and his dog Ripper (named after his hero Cal Ripken) and relaxed by playing golf and boating on the Atlantic Ocean.

On Christmas morning 2000, A-Rod's mom, Lourdes, gave him a meaningful present: a book about Leonardo da Vinci, whom A-Rod had admired since he was a little boy. Also during the holidays, A-Rod and his entire family went to the Dominican Republic. When they returned home, A-Rod had a party with his friends and family to celebrate his buying a new boat, appropriately named *Sweet Swing*. He docked the boat near his home in Miami.

But soon it was time to get back to work. Since he was the highest-paid athlete in professional sports, A-Rod knew that expectations for him were sky high. Former teammate Ken Griffey Jr.

cautioned him that he was in for his "most challenging year."

He was up for the challenge. Tom Hicks, the Rangers' owner, was determined that his team would win a world championship. Hicks had already purchased the Dallas Stars hockey team and helped make them Stanley Cup champions. He was willing to spend money on the right players to help get the Rangers to the World Series.

Along with A-Rod, other major batters on the Rangers team included All-Star catcher Ivan "Pudge" Rodriguez, who'd hit .347 in 2000, and first baseman Rafael Palmeiro, a powerhouse home-run hitter. Where the Rangers were weak was in their pitching. But despite Hicks's efforts, no star pitchers were interested in joining the Rangers. Without a strong pitching staff, it would be hard to be real competitors.

Still, when A-Rod showed up for spring training in Port Charlotte, Florida, he was determined to make 2001 a great season. He could barely believe the crowds who came out to see him. People swarmed him for photos and autographs. As always, A-Rod was polite and chatted with fans. Like his idol Cal Ripken, he knew the importance of being a good person and not just a great player. He didn't take any of the attention for granted.

When the 2001 season started, A-Rod was fired up and ready to go. The Rangers opened the season by traveling to San Juan, Puerto Rico, to play the Toronto Blue Jays. (Major League

Baseball likes to send its teams to different parts of the world to expose new fans to the game.) A-Rod was nervous but excited.

In the first inning, he got a base hit. But things got worse from there. First he fielded a grounder but wildly threw the ball past first base. Then, when trying to execute a double play, the twenty-five-year-old tripped on his own shoelaces and fell. The Rangers lost 8–1. "You have to start somewhere," A-Rod said after the game. "[The game] had a little of everything—error, slip, hit. . . . You just move on."

❝*I don't take any of it to heart.***❞**

—ALEX RODRIGUEZ, ON CRITICISM
THAT HIS $252-MILLION SALARY WAS TOO HIGH

In mid-April, A-Rod and the Rangers headed to Seattle to play their first game against the Mariners. A-Rod didn't exactly get the welcome of an old friend. Instead he faced boos and hisses from fans who felt he'd betrayed the Mariners by leaving them. But A-Rod wasn't angry about the cold reception. He understood the Mariners fans' disappointment.

By May the Rangers slipped in the standings and had lost fourteen out of twenty-five games. The front office decided it was time to shake things up and replaced manager Johnny Oates with Jerry Narron. That change gave the guys on the team a morale boost. Then A-Rod helped things when he got his 1,000th career hit off pitcher Gary Glover of the Chicago White Sox.

In July A-Rod was once again part of the All-Star game. This time he switched positions so that his idol Cal Ripken could play shortstop in his final All-Star game before retiring. A-Rod happily took third base. Even although the game was played in Seattle, that generous gesture gave A-Rod a round of cheers from the fans in the stands.

In September A-Rod hit his 48th home run of the season off Anaheim Angel Ramon Ortiz. With that achievement, he bypassed Chicago Cubs legend Ernie Banks for the most homers in a season by a shortstop. Banks sent Alex a message: "Congratulations to A-Rod. I knew you could do it. You are a great man, an impressive baseball player, and a role model. I love the game of baseball, and I love to see players with heart and drive like yours who continue the spirit of the game."

Despite A-Rod's winning play, the Rangers had a less-than-impressive season. They ended with a record of 73 wins and 89 losses and landed in last place in the American League West.

But A-Rod had lived up to management's expectations. He had hit .318, played in all 162 games, led the American League in home runs (he had hit 52 by season's end), and had 135 RBIs and 201 hits. He also became the fourth player ever (and the first since Detroit Tiger Jimmie Foxx in 1932) to hit more than 50 home runs and collect 200 hits in a single season. Although A-Rod didn't get picked as the American League's MVP (the Seattle Mariners' new outfielder Ichiro Suzuki won, and A-Rod finished in sixth place in the voting), he was honored with the Hank Aaron Award as the AL's best hitter.

"Alex has played tremendously well," said teammate Gabe Kapler. "We've gotten everything we could have possibly hoped for from Alex Rodriguez." And one major league scout raved, "His team scuffled but he still dived for balls even when his team was down 10–1. He plays hard all the time. He plays the game right."

 In 2001 A-Rod was named one of *People* magazine's "50 Most Beautiful People in the

Meanwhile the Mariners had a great season. They won 116 games and made the playoffs. It was a bittersweet time for A-Rod.

But Rangers owner Tom Hicks was determined to craft a better team for the 2002 season. In December he brought on board star pitchers Chan Ho Park and John Rocker and hitter Carl Everett. Outfielder Juan Gonzalez was re-signed to a two-year deal. When A-Rod showed up for spring training in February, he felt very optimistic about the team.

At the end of April, A-Rod hit his 250th home run. The twenty-six-year-old became the second-youngest player (behind Jimmie Foxx) to reach that mark. He was playing well, and in June he was elected to the All-Star team for the fifth year in a row. On his twenty-seventh birthday, on July 27, he hit a grand slam, his 34th homer of the season. And in a series against Toronto in September, A-Rod hit six homers in three games. He was only the fourth player in the history of major league baseball to reach that milestone.

But his team wasn't following suit. The Rangers finished the season with a 72–90 record. They were last in the American League West for the second season in a row.

Although his team had crumbled, A-Rod had shone during the season. He led both leagues with 57 home runs (the second-highest total for a right-handed hitter in American League history), 142 RBIs, and 389 total bases and became the first player to lead the majors in all three categories since Tony Armas of the Boston Red Sox had done it in 1984. He had also hit .300 and driven in 142 runs.

In the past, A-Rod had never publicly expressed his desire to be voted the league's Most Valuable Player. But this time he was verbal about his hopes. "Sure, I'd be disappointed if I'm not the MVP," he said. "I've been in the race a few times. I've come close. I deserve it."

But Oakland A's shortstop Miguel Tejada was chosen MVP, and A-Rod came in second place. Tejada came in ahead of A-Rod, many thought, because the A's had made the playoffs and the Rangers hadn't even been in contention.

A-Rod had to put that loss behind him. He had other things to focus on. He continued working on his charitable efforts. In October he made a $3.9-million contribution to the baseball program at the University of Miami, the school he'd almost attended. Most of the money went toward renovating the baseball stadium he used to sneak into as a child. "This is my Yankee Stadium, my Candlestick Park, my Dodger Stadium," A-Rod said at the opening ceremony for the new stadium. "I used to jump the fence. They had high trees over there. I fell a few times, but I still got in. I remember being sad on Sundays when the sun went down because I had to wait another week to see the [University of Miami] Hurricanes play." A-Rod also revealed to the press that he wanted to return to the school one day to get his bachelor's degree in literature.

A-Rod had another big moment on November 2, 2002. He married his longtime sweetheart Cynthia Scurtis in a private wedding ceremony, held at a home A-Rod had purchased in the Highland Park section of Dallas. Cal Ripken was one of the guests.

Later that month, A-Rod got a boost in his career when he was honored with his first-ever Gold Glove award, thanks to his supreme performance on the field: only 10 errors in 741 chances. The Gold Glove is awarded to the league's best fielder at each position.

A-Rod loves hip-hop music (Jay-Z is one of his favorite artists), singer Mariah Carey, and the legendary rock group the Rolling Stones.

In February 2003, A-Rod headed for spring training in Surprise, Arizona. Changes were afoot. Manager Jerry Narron had been replaced with former Yankee and Arizona Diamondback manager Buck Showalter. Pitchers Ugueth Urbina and Esteban Yan were also brought on board.

But on his first day of playing in training, A-Rod felt a stabbing pain above his shoulders. He went to the doctor and was diagnosed with a herniated (ruptured) disk in his neck. Luckily he was healed by the time the season opened against the Anaheim Angels on April 2, 2003. In this game, he hit his 300th career home run off pitcher Ramon Ortiz, becoming the youngest player (twenty-seven years, 249 days) to achieve that honor.

Once again, though, the Rangers were in trouble. By the end of May, they were heading to last place. Owner Tom Hicks even began trading away some of the team's higher-priced players to give some rookies a chance.

By the end of July, after A-Rod was again selected to play in the All-Star game, the Rangers were losing regularly. At a press conference, A-Rod said he wanted to be part of a winning team that could make it to the World Series.

A-Rod's words seemed to spark his teammates. By August the team had an improved record of 57 wins and 57 losses. But that improvement was short-lived. By September the Rangers were in a slump, and A-Rod did something he'd never done: he broke his streak of playing 546 games in a row and sat out a game in frustration.

By season's end, the Rangers had a 71–91 record, finishing in last place in the American League West and 25 games behind the division-winning Oakland A's. The Rangers' pitching hadn't been strong enough, and the lineup hadn't been powerful.

But A-Rod had definitely done his part for the team. He had hit .298, won the American League home-run title for the third year in a row with 47 home runs, finished the season with a league-high 124 runs, and made only 8 errors in 158 games. But A-Rod's great season personally didn't change the fact that he was playing for a losing team.

His contributions would be recognized, though. In November he was given the Gold Glove, the Silver Slugger Award, and the Hank Aaron Award. On November 18, 2003, he was named the Most Valuable Player in the American League, beating out Carlos Delgado of the Toronto Blue Jays. It was a huge achievement, one he had been wanting for a long time.

Alex had a lot on his mind. When he spoke to reporters after winning the MVP honors, he said he felt "humbled and overwhelmed." But he also admitted that he would approve a trade if it allowed him to go to a winning team. He had to decide whether to stay with Texas or go elsewhere.

Chapter Nine

Blue-and-White Stripes

O nce A-Rod made it known that he would consider being traded from the Texas Rangers, it didn't take long for the Boston Red Sox to come calling. They had just lost the American League Championship Series to the New York Yankees, and they were willing to swap outfielder Manny Ramirez for A-Rod. Rangers owner Tom Hicks was having financial trouble, and even though Ramirez was also a high-priced player, his contract was shorter than A-Rod's. So if the Rangers traded A-Rod for Ramirez, they would save almost $100 million in the long run.

A-Rod's wife, Cynthia, had relatives in the Boston area, and Fenway Park, where the Red Sox played, was rich in history. A-Rod liked the idea of playing there. Plus he felt the Red Sox could finally take him to the World Series. For A-Rod the team seemed like a perfect match.

But the New York Yankees were also interested in A-Rod. They already had a top shortstop, Derek Jeter. But their third baseman, Aaron Boone, had badly injured his ankle in a game of pickup basketball and would have to sit out the entire season. The Yankees wanted A-Rod on board as their new third baseman, if he would agree to switch positions.

---

66 *I look at it as a new challenge. I achieved just about everything personally at shortstop. Now it's time to win. I've always thought of myself as a team player. Playing third base is the ultimate team move.* 99

—A-ROD, ON SWITCHING TO THIRD BASE

Meanwhile, because of Major League Baseball Players Association regulations, the deal with the Red Sox fell through. A-Rod didn't know what was going to happen next. In early February, he returned to Texas as the new Rangers team captain. Although he admitted his frustration, A-Rod told reporters that following a five-hour discussion with team owner Tom Hicks and manager Buck Showalter, he felt the team had some hope for the 2004 season.

"After that meeting, I felt like the Rangers had a great plan in hand," said A-Rod. "I felt very comfortable about where the

Texas Rangers were heading. As long as the train was moving forward and in the right direction, that was all I wanted to see."

Although it appeared A-Rod had returned to the Rangers, the rumor in the sports world was that he was going to become a Yankee. On February 15, 2004, the story broke: Texas was trading A-Rod for Yankee Alfonso Soriano. Rangers owner Tom Hicks had made the decision. "My baseball experts gave me their advice," Hicks said, "and it was that we can build a championship team faster here in Texas by doing this trade today."

For A-Rod, becoming a Yankee was an incredible feeling. He was joining the most successful team in baseball history. A-Rod accepted the position of third baseman, and Derek Jeter would continue on as shortstop. "I think we will make a great tag team," A-Rod said during the press conference at Yankee Stadium announcing the trade. "Derek is a 'great' here. . . . I want to learn from him and play under his leadership."

Wow! What a reception. I feel overwhelmed and very, very happy to be here.

—A-ROD'S FIRST WORDS AS A NEW YORK YANKEE, AT A FEBRUARY 2004 PRESS CONFERENCE

During the day of the press conference, Alex was treated like royalty. As he drove away from Yankee Stadium, he saw a huge sign on the side of the building. It read, "A-Rod, Welcome to NY." Then he and wife Cynthia met Mayor Michael Bloomberg in city hall. One of their last stops on that whirlwind day was to look at apartments. Less than a week later, A-Rod suited up and joined the Yankees in spring training at Legends Field in Tampa, Florida.

In March A-Rod was amazed by the spectacle before the Yankees' first spring-training game. Fireworks, parachutists, and Yankee greats including Reggie Jackson, Whitey Ford, and Yogi Berra were all a part of the lavish pregame celebration. A-Rod had to pinch himself. "When you see all the [Yankee] Hall of Famers lining up," he said, "it's hard not to get caught up in the moment."

After the game against the Philadelphia Phillies, which the Yankees won 7–5, A-Rod said that playing for the Yankees felt like a dream. "When I was rounding third, I asked myself, 'Where am I?' I felt like I was in Disney World," he told reporters.

A-Rod had a scare during a spring-training matchup against the Boston Red Sox on March 24. Yankee left fielder Hideki Matsui threw a ball that ricocheted off the leg of a slid-ing base runner and then hit A-Rod in the face. Luckily he ended up with only a welt under his eye.

When the season started, the Yanks traveled to Japan to play the Tampa Bay Devil Rays. For once A-Rod wasn't the man in the spotlight. Instead Matsui, a Japanese native nicknamed

Godzilla, got all the attention back in his homeland. Although the Yankees lost to the D-Rays 8–3, A-Rod had a good game, hitting a double and scoring a run.

A-Rod gave Yankees first baseman—and former Seattle Mariners teammate—Tino Martinez a nickname, the Bridge, for helping link him to the other Yankees on the team.

A-Rod was thrilled and awed to be part of the legendary Yankees, and he wrote about it in a cover story for *ESPN the Magazine*. "I honestly feel like I'm on another planet," he wrote. "You go from three straight years of last place to this, and it's like breathing a different kind of air."

On April 6, A-Rod hit his first home run as a Yankee during another game against the Devil Rays. The next day, A-Rod fielded a slick play. He fired a ground ball hit by the D-Rays' Brook Fordyce over to first base and helped win the game 3–2.

Then on April 8, he played his first game at Yankee Stadium. A-Rod scored a run, helping the Yanks beat the Chicago White Sox 3–1. He was cheered by fans, who were happy to have him on board as their third baseman.

LUCKY 13

Starting in high school, A-Rod always wore number 3 on his baseball uniform. But he couldn't wear 3 as a Yankee because the Yankees had retired the number (no longer used it) after the legendary hitter Babe Ruth (also number 3) left the team. So A-Rod added a 1 to Ruth's number and chose number 13 for his Yankees jersey. Thirteen also happened to be the number worn by one of A-Rod's childhood idols, Dan Marino of the Miami Dolphins football

But it was a much different story when the team headed to Fenway Park on April 16 to play the Boston Red Sox. Red Sox fans were still smarting from the fact that they'd almost had A-Rod on their team. They resented him for not coming to play for Boston, even though it wasn't his fault that negotiations between the Texas Rangers and the Red Sox had fallen apart. Add the fact that the Yankees and the Sox are the biggest rivals in baseball, and A-Rod was on Boston's list of enemies.

During batting practice, one Red Sox fan yelled to him, "Hey, A-Rod! What's it like to be Jeter's backup?"—implying that as third baseman, A-Rod was less important than star shortstop Derek Jeter. And every time A-Rod came to the plate during the game, the Boston fans booed. "It was pretty intense out there," he said afterwards. "The fans here are always intense and rabid. Tonight was as loud as I've heard it."

Though he tried hard not to be affected by all the negativity toward him, Alex struggled in Boston. In the series against the Red Sox, he went 1 for 17 (one hit in seventeen at bats), and his batting average dropped to .160. When he grounded out during a game on April 17, he slammed down his helmet. Later A-Rod said it felt good to vent. "Sometimes you need to let it out, let the frustration out," he said. "When you've been stinking up the place like I have lately, the focus is definitely to let out some emotion."

Things started turning around for A-Rod when he hit his second homer as a Yankee during an April 21 game against the White Sox. Then on May 4, in a game against the Oakland A's, he hit his 350th career homer. He became the 70th player to reach that goal and the youngest in major league history (twenty-eight years, 282 days). "This is my biggest hit as a Yankee," he said.

A-Rod faced a tough crowd once again when he returned to Arlington, Texas, on May 21 to play the Texas Rangers. He was booed by fans who felt he'd abandoned their team to go to the Yankees. But at his first at bat, he hit a two-run homer and even managed to get some cheers from the sold-out crowd.

Yankees manager Joe Torre admired A-Rod's sense of team spirit. "He's a very respectful guy," he said. "The one thing is, I don't care how big a star he is, or how much money he makes. . . . He's a hard worker."

By mid-June, A-Rod was batting .305 with 14 home runs and 36 RBIs. He was adjusting to being a Yankee and facing all the pressures of being on baseball's most visible team. On June 22, he passed Yankee legend Joe DiMaggio on the career-home-run list when he slammed his 363rd home run in a double-homer game against the Baltimore Orioles.

But on July 24, things got ugly in a game against the Boston Red Sox. In the top of the third inning at Fenway Park, Sox pitcher Bronson Arroyo hit A-Rod with a pitch. As the Yankee walked toward first base, he stared down Arroyo. Sox catcher Jason Varitek got between the two, and a pushing match broke out. Before long both teams were involved in the brawl. Ultimately A-Rod and Varitek were both suspended for four games and fined $2,000.

With that incident behind him, A-Rod put his focus back on his game. In a July 31 matchup against the Baltimore Orioles, he hit his 27th home run of the season. A month later, on September 6, Yankees manager Joe Torre decided to move A-Rod to the number-two spot in the batting order, right behind Derek Jeter.

In the second game of a September 29 doubleheader against the Minnesota Twins, A-Rod powered a two-run triple in the seventh inning and then smacked his 36th homer of the season. "This is the best I've felt all year," said Alex. The Yankees were feeling pretty good too. With several key hits, A-Rod helped them win all three games of a three-game series against the Minnesota Twins.

Many people compare A-Rod to the legendary Yankee Babe Ruth. They even call him the Latin Babe Ruth.

When the regular season ended, the Yankees were in first place in their division, the AL East, with a 101–61 record. It was a satisfying feeling for A-Rod, who'd been so frustrated not making it to the postseason with the Texas Rangers.

In the ALDS, the Yankees faced the Minnesota Twins. The Yankees had beat the Twins just five days earlier, so they had a lot of confidence going into the series. But in game one, the Twins beat the Yanks on their home turf—Yankee Stadium. Game two was tied after nine innings, and by the bottom of the twelfth, the Twins were leading 6–5. A-Rod came to bat with one out and runners on first and second. He smacked a line drive to left-center field, and the ball bounced over the fence for a ground-rule double. One runner scored, tying the game. A-Rod was still on second base later in the inning when Derek

Jeter scored the winning run. The series headed to Minnesota for games three and four. The Yankees dominated game three, winning 8–4, and then battled for eleven innings to win game four, 6–5, with A-Rod scoring the winning run.

In the ALCS, the Yanks' opponents were their historic rivals—the Boston Red Sox. New York started off strong, winning games one and two. After winning game three 19–8, thanks in part to an A-Rod home run, the Yankees seemed sure to sweep the series. No team had ever blown a three-game lead to lose a seven-game postseason series. But incredibly, Boston won games four and five in extra innings.

A particularly low point for A-Rod came during game six. He was called out for interference when he ran to first base and slapped down on the arm of Sox pitcher Bronson Arroyo, who had picked up the ball near the foul line and was running to tag him out. "This is obviously crushing for us," A-Rod told reporters about the devastating ALCS loss. "I don't have words for the disappointment." The Yankees couldn't pull themselves together after three devastating losses, and the Red Sox won game seven and the pennant.

A-Rod accomplished a lot during his first season with the Yankees. He hit .286 with 36 home runs and 106 RBIs. He also became one of only three players in major league history to bring in at least 35 homers, 100 runs scored, and 100 RBIs in seven consecutive seasons. (The others were Babe Ruth and Jimmie Foxx.)

The Boston Red Sox went on to sweep the St. Louis Cardinals in the 2004 World Series, claiming their first world championship in eighty-six years.

Still, the star third baseman felt he and the Yankees could have accomplished more. "The fact that I haven't won a championship bothers me," he said. "Until I do, I will not sleep or be comfortable with my career."

Chapter Ten

Mr. 400

After the Yanks' disappointing performance in the ALCS, A-Rod was excited about a new development in his life. On November 18, 2004, his wife Cynthia gave birth to their first child, daughter Natasha Alexander. Becoming a father was thrilling to A-Rod. He wanted to help Natasha grow and learn. Most important, he wanted to be there to nurture her.

In February 2005, A-Rod returned to Tampa, Florida, for spring training. The season began on March 3. Off the field, A-Rod had a heroic moment on April 12. As he was waiting at a crosswalk in Boston, he saw eight-year-old Patrick McCarthy start running across the street. A-Rod pulled Patrick back to the curb, out of the path of an oncoming truck.

On the field, A-Rod was also doing well. In an April 27 game against the Los Angeles Angels (who changed their name from the Anaheim Angels), he hit three homers in his first three at bats and helped his team to a 12–4 victory. "Tonight was one of those magical nights. It felt like I was in the clouds—you just don't want it to end," he said of his performance before 36,328 wildly cheering fans at Yankee Stadium. "I've hit three home runs twice before, but nothing feels as special as this, doing it in New York, doing it in the pinstripes [Yankees uniform]." He also became only the eleventh major league player with ten or more RBIs in a game.

A-Rod doesn't take a limousine to home games like some players. He prefers to drive himself. "[Driving is] my personal time to prepare for the game or wind down from it," he says.

In May A-Rod led the league in home runs, RBIs, and runs and was also named Player of the Month. In early June, he admitted something personal to reporters. He said he had been seeing a therapist to resolve issues from his childhood. The most difficult problem he had faced was his father abandoning the family when Alex was so young. Alex wanted kids everywhere to know that even a sports star can use help sometimes. "What's happening with little kids in today's generation is a lot of suicide, a lot of mental problems going on, and a lot of it is because they think therapy is a real bad thing," he said. "And it's not. And that's why I came out and said it's been very helpful in my personal life."

Just days later, on June 8, A-Rod reached a milestone when he powered his 400th home run against the Milwaukee Brewers. By the end of July, he was batting .318 and was happy about his position with the team.

❝ *He is baseball twenty-four hours a day. When we were kids, he'd make me meet him at the park at 5:30 in the morning. I'd be half asleep, and he'd be like, 'O.K., drills!'* ❞

—GUI SOCCARAS, LONGTIME A-ROD PAL

Things just kept improving. On August 30, in a game against the Seattle Mariners, he became the first right-handed Yankee batter to hit 40 home runs in a season since Joe DiMaggio hit 46 in 1937. On September 24, A-Rod tied with DiMaggio with his 46th home run of the season. Four days later, he hit his 47th homer.

Then on October 1, in the fifth inning of an American League East title game with the Boston Red Sox, a knuckle ball from Sox pitcher Tim Wakefield came A-Rod's way. Connecting with that pitch, he scored his 48th home run of the season. It tied him with Adrian Beltre and Mike Schmidt for most homers in a season for a third baseman. To top it off, the Yankees won the AL East title with an 8–4 victory over the Sox.

A-Rod's teammates were full of praise about their third baseman, who had four hits in the game. "What can you say about a performance like that," designated hitter Jason Giambi said about A-Rod. "It's good to have him up near the top of the lineup because he can set things up for guys like me and [Gary Sheffield]. And I've always said, every time he comes up he's in scoring position."

❝*I like playing at the Stadium. I like hitting at the Stadium. I feel like I'm home.***❞**

—ALEX ON PLAYING AT YANKEE STADIUM

Hopes were high when the Yankees faced the Los Angeles Angels in the best-of-five-game ALDS. After winning the first game with a score of 4–2 and losing the next two, the Yankees forced a fifth game when they defeated the Angels 3–2 on October 9.

But the following night, during game five, the Yanks had an embarrassing moment in the second inning. Bubba Crosby and

Gary Sheffield collided against the wall as they both ran for the ball. Ultimately the Yankees lost 5–3 and squelched their chance of competing against the Chicago White Sox in the ALCS.

GIVE A HAND

In the spring of 2005, A-Rod and his wife, Cynthia, donated $200,000 to a children's mental health center in Washington Heights, the New York City neighborhood where A-Rod was born.

A-Rod was especially upset about his performance in the ALDS. In the sixth inning of game two, he had fumbled a grounder, a mistake that contributed to the Yankees' loss. And he'd hit 2 for 15 with a .133 average and no RBIs during the series. "I played great baseball all year and I played like a dog for five days," Alex told reporters. The third baseman even apologized to Yankees coaches for grounding out into a double play in the ninth inning of game five.

But despite his lackluster postseason play, A-Rod had still had a fantastic sophomore season as a Yankee. He had a .321 average, 130 RBIs, 194 hits, 48 home runs, and 21 stolen bases.

And once he let the crushing disappointment of the ALDS loss settle in, he felt optimistic about the 2006 season. "I still believe we're the best team in baseball," he said. "I'll always think that. You can't question our effort." The same can be said for A-Rod, who always gives his all.

Epilogue

A Living Legend

Although Alex Rodriguez didn't play in the 2005 World
Series, he still received a special honor there. On
October 26, before game four of the series, A-Rod walked on
the field at the Houston Astrodome to be named a member of the
"Latino Legends" baseball team, along with such greats as
the late Roberto Clemente, Juan Marichal, and Rod Carew.
A-Rod was proud to be admired as one of the best Latino players in baseball. "It's just a tremendous honor," he said. "It's a
treat. It's pretty special."

In the series, the Chicago White Sox walked away world
champions. Soon after, talk turned to the MVP race. Many won-
dered whether A-Rod had a shot at becoming the American
League MVP for the second time in his career.

White Sox manager Ozzie Guillen made the case for why
A-Rod should win the honor over the other leading contender,

Red Sox designated hitter David Ortiz: "[A-Rod] steals bases, goes from first to third, makes all the plays on defense, gets the big hits," Guillen said. "He can beat you so many [more] ways than Ortiz." Yankees teammate Randy Johnson added, "Alex is the MVP. I've seen him save countless games with his defense and win countless games with his offense."

The good news came on November 14, 2005, when thirty-year-old Alex Rodriguez was indeed named American League Most Valuable Player. The award put a positive spin on the end of a roller coaster of a season. Yankees owner George Steinbrenner praised his MVP. "A-Rod demonstrates the talent, hard work, and dedication of a true winner," he said. But A-Rod admitted, "I would certainly trade [David Ortiz's 2004] World Series championship for this MVP trophy. [Winning the World Series is] the only reason I play baseball. It's what I'm consumed to do right now."

It's clear that until he becomes a world champion, A-Rod won't be satisfied. Winning the World Series has been his quest since he started playing baseball as a little boy in the Dominican Republic. This goal has driven him to succeed in the major leagues. He'll continue to work hard both at the plate and on the field until he gets his World Series ring. "I have five years left on this contract, and that's a lot of baseball. I take the game so [seriously]. I commit myself so much," he has said.

A-Rod is also committed to being a good husband and father and a positive role model for all his fans. "We must always strive to do the right thing," he once wrote. "In my case, that means playing hard and honorably. In doing so, I honor all those people who have supported me throughout my life."

PERSONAL STATISTICS

Name:

Alexander Emmanuel Rodriguez

Nickname:

A-Rod

Born:

July 27, 1975

Height:

6'3"

Weight:

225 lbs.

Bats:

Right

Throws:

Right

BATTING STATISTICS

Year	Team	Avg	G	AB	Runs	Hits	2B	3B	HR	RBI	SB
1994	SEA	0.204	17	54	4	11	0	0	0	2	3
1995	SEA	0.232	48	142	15	33	6	2	5	19	4
1996	SEA	0.358	146	601	141	215	54	1	36	123	15
1997	SEA	0.300	141	587	100	176	40	3	23	84	29
1998	SEA	0.310	161	686	123	213	35	5	42	124	46
1999	SEA	0.285	129	502	110	143	25	0	42	111	21
2000	SEA	0.316	148	554	134	175	34	2	41	132	15
2001	TEX	0.318	162	632	133	201	34	1	52	135	18
2002	TEX	0.300	162	624	125	187	27	2	57	142	9
2003	TEX	0.298	161	607	124	181	30	6	47	118	17
2004	NYY	0.286	155	601	112	172	24	2	36	106	28
2005	NYY	0.321	162	605	124	194	29	1	48	130	21
	Totals	0.307	1,592	6,195	1,245	1,901	338	25	429	1,226	226

Key: **Avg**: batting average; **G**: games; **AB**: at bats; **2B**: doubles; **3B**: triples; **HR**: home runs; **RBI**: runs batted in; **SB**: stolen bases

FIELDING STATISTICS

Year	Team	Pos	G	C	PO	A	E	DP	FLD%
1994	SEA	SS	17	71	20	45	6	9	0.915
1995	SEA	SS	46	169	56	106	8	14	0.953
1996	SEA	SS	146	657	238	403	15	92	0.977
1997	SEA	SS	140	628	209	394	24	85	0.962
1998	SEA	SS	160	736	268	447	18	89	0.976
1999	SEA	SS	129	611	213	383	14	103	0.977
2000	SEA	SS	148	690	242	438	10	122	0.986
2001	TEX	SS	161	749	280	451	18	117	0.976
2002	TEX	SS	162	741	259	472	10	108	0.987
2003	TEX	SS	158	699	227	464	8	111	0.989
2004	NYY	3B	155	375	100	262	13	25	0.965
2004	NYY	SS	2	2	1	1	0	1	1.000
2005	NYY	3B	161	415	115	288	12	26	0.971
2005	NYY	SS	3	3	1	2	0	0	1.000
Total as 3B			316	790	215	550	25	51	0.968
Total as SS			1,272	5,756	2,014	3,606	131	851	0.977

Key: Pos: position; G: games; C: chances (balls hit to a position); PO: putouts; A: assists; E: errors; DP: double plays; FLD%: fielding percentage

BIBLIOGRAPHY

BOOKS

Bradley, Michael. *Alex Rodriguez.* New York: Benchmark Books, 2005.

Christopher, Matt. *On the Field with . . . Alex Rodriguez.* New York: Little, Brown and Co., 2002.

Fitzgerald, James. *A-Rod: Major League Hero.* New York: Penguin Group, 2004.

Gallagher, Jim. *Alex Rodriguez.* Bear, DE: Mitchell Lane Publishers, 2000.

Rodriguez, Alex, with Greg Brown. *Alex Rodriguez: Hit a Grand Slam!* Dallas: Taylor Publishing Co., 1998.

SELECTED NEWSPAPER AND MAGAZINE ARTICLES

Anthony, Mike. "Satisfying Turn for A-Rod; Puts to Rest Nightmares of First Season with Yankees." *Hartford Courant (Connecticut)*, October 2, 2005.

Blum, Ronald. "Rodriguez Beats Ortiz to Win Second MVP in Three Seasons." Associated Press, November 14, 2005.

Cafardo, Nick. "A-Rod Introduced to Rivalry." *Boston Globe*, April 17, 2004.

Costello, Brian. "My Bad! A-Rod Apologized to Coaching Staff Following Game Five." *New York Post*, October 13, 2005.

Curry, Jack. "Rodriguez Is Haunted by Yanks' Collapse." *New York Times*, November 14, 2004.

De Luca, Chris. "Alex in Wonderland." *Chicago Sun-Times*, April 8, 2004.

Gonzales, Mark. "City Slicker; A-Rod Slowly Warms to a New York State of Mind." *Arizona Republic (Phoenix)*, June 15, 2004.

O'Brien, Kathleen. "A-Rod Turns into A-Clod in ALCS." *Fort Worth Star-Telegram*, October 22, 2004.

Reilly, Rick. "A Gentleman in a Pinstripe Suit." *Sports Illustrated*, July 12–19, 2004.

WEB SITES

AROD.com

www.arod.com

A-Rod's official site includes news headlines, stats, a photo gallery, a journal, and more.

Baseball-Reference.com

www.baseball-reference.com/r/rodrial01.shtml

This site includes A-Rod's complete batting and fielding statistics, awards he's won, and comparisons to other players.

ESPN.com

http://sports.espn.go.com/mlb/players/profile?statsId=5275

The sports-channel site offers stats, scouting report information, and articles on the Yankee third baseman.

New York Yankees: The Official Site

www.yankees.com

This site is a great resource for everything you want to know about A-Rod's team.

INDEX